THE RAINBOW OF SORROW

*The Seven Last Words and
The Art of Understanding
Pain and Suffering*

FULTON J. SHEEN

Bishop Sheen Today
280 John Street
Midland, Ontario, Canada
L4R 2J5

www.bishopsheentoday.com

Library of Congress Cataloging-in-Publication Data

Names: Sheen, Fulton J. (Fulton John), 1895-1979, author. | Smith, Allan J., editor.

Sheen, Fulton J. (Fulton John), 1895-1979. The Rainbow of Sorrow. – Registered in the name of P.J. Kenedy & Sons, under Library of Congress catalog card number: A116722 following publication April 14, 1938.

Smith, Al (Allan J.) editor – The Cries of Jesus from the Cross: A Fulton Sheen Anthology. Manchester, New Hampshire: Sophia Institute Press, 2018, ISBN 9781622826209.

Title: The Rainbow of Sorrow: The Seven Last Words and the Art of Understanding Pain and Suffering

Fulton J. Sheen; compiled by Allan J. Smith.

Description: Midland, Ontario: Bishop Sheen Today, 2021

Includes bibliographical references.

Identifiers:
ISBN: 978-1-998229-38-3 (paperback)
ISBN: 978-1-7371890-2-2 (eBook)
ISBN: 978-1-990427-76-3 (hardcover)

Subjects: Jesus Christ — The Seven Last Words — Pain — Suffering

DEDICATED TO

The Mother of Sorrows

TO WHOM THE SEVEN WORDS
FROM THE CROSS WERE AS
THE SEVEN RAINBOW COLORS
FROM THE SKY:

A PLEDGE OF THE END OF
THE DELUGE OF PAIN
IN THE GLORY OF THE RISEN CHRIST
THE LIGHT OF THE WORLD

*Ad maiorem Dei gloriam
inque hominum salutem*

Jesus calls all His children to the pulpit of the Cross, and every word He says to them is set down for the purpose of an eternal publication and undying consolation.

There was never a preacher like the dying Christ.

There was never a congregation like that which gathered about the pulpit of the Cross.

And there was never a sermon like the Seven Last Words.

Archbishop Fulton J. Sheen

THE SEVEN LAST WORDS OF CHRIST

The First Word
"Father, Forgive Them For They

Know Not What They Do."

The Second Word
"This Day Thou Shalt Be

With Me In Paradise."

The Third Word
"Woman, Behold Thy Son;

Behold Thy Mother."

The Fourth Word
"My God! My God!

Why Hast Thou Forsaken Me?"

The Fifth Word
"I Thirst."

The Sixth Word
"It Is Finished."

The Seventh Word
"Father, Into Thy Hands

I Commend My Spirit."

CONTENTS

PREFACE

"I have learned more from the crucifix than from any book."
St. Thomas Aquinas

ARCHBISHOP FULTON J. SHEEN was a man for all seasons. Over his lifetime, he spent himself for souls, transforming lives with the clear teaching of the truths of Christ and His Church through his books, his radio addresses, his lectures, his television series, and his many newspaper columns.

The topics of this much-sought-after lecturer ranged from the social concerns of the day to matters of faith and morals. With an easy and personable manner, Sheen could strike up a conversation on just about any subject, making numerous friends as well as converts.

During the 1930s and '40s, Fulton Sheen was the featured speaker on The Catholic Hour radio broadcast, and millions of listeners heard his radio addresses each week. His topics ranged from politics and the economy to philosophy and man's eternal pursuit of happiness.

Along with his weekly radio program, Sheen wrote dozens of books and pamphlets.

One can safely say that through his writings, thousands of people changed their perspectives about God and the Church. Sheen was quoted as saying, "There are not one hundred people in the United States who hate the Catholic Church, but there are millions who hate what they wrongly perceive the Catholic Church to be."

Possessing a burning zeal to dispel the myths about Our Lord and His Church, Sheen gave a series of powerful presentations on Christ's Passion and His seven last words from the Cross. As a Scripture scholar, Archbishop Sheen knew full well the power contained in preaching Christ crucified. With St. Paul, he could say, "For I decided to know nothing among you except Jesus Christ and him crucified" (1 Cor. 2:2).

During his last recorded Good Friday address in 1979, Archbishop Sheen spoke of having given this type of reflection on the subject of Christ's seven last words from the Cross "for the fifty-eighth consecutive time." Whether from the young priest in Peoria, Illinois, the university professor in Washington, D.C., or the bishop in New York, Sheen's messages were sure to make an indelible mark on his listeners.

Given their importance and the impact they had on society, it seemed appropriate to bring back this collection of Sheen's radio addresses that were later compiled into a book titled *The Rainbow of Sorrow* (New York: P.J. Kenedy and Sons, 1938).

On October 2, 1979, when visiting St. Patrick's Cathedral in New York City, Pope John Paul II embraced Fulton Sheen and spoke into his ear a blessing and an affirmation. He said: "You have written and spoken well of the Lord Jesus Christ. You are a loyal son of the Church." On the day Archbishop Sheen died (December 9, 1979), he was found in his private chapel before the Eucharist in the shadow of the cross. Archbishop Sheen was a man purified in the fires of love and by the wood of the Cross.

It is hoped that, upon reading these reflections, the reader will concur with the heartfelt affirmation given by St. John Paul II and countless others of Sheen's wisdom and fidelity. May these writings by Archbishop Fulton J. Sheen evoke in the reader a greater love and understanding of the pain and suffering present in the world today.

UNJUST SUFFERING

(The First Word from the Cross)

"Father, forgive them, for they know not what they do."

THE WORLD IS FULL OF those who suffer unjustly and who through no fault of their own bear the "slings and arrows of outrageous fortune." What should be our attitude to those who speak untruly of us, who malign our good names, who steal our reputations, and who sneer at our acts of kindness?

The answer is to be found in the first word from the Cross: *forgive.* If there was ever anyone who had a right to protest against injustice it was He Who is Divine Justice; if ever there was anyone who was entitled to reproach those who dug His hands and feet with steel, it was Our Lord on the Cross.

And yet, at that very moment when a tree turns against Him and becomes a cross, when iron turns against Him and becomes nails, when roses turn against Him and become thorns, when men turn against Him and become executioners, He lets fall from His lips for the first time in the history of the world a prayer for enemies: "Father, forgive them, for they know not what they do" *(Luke 23:34)*.

Dwell for a moment on what He did not say. He did not say: "I am innocent," and yet who else could have better claimed innocence? Many times before this Good Friday and many times since, men have been sent to a cross, a guillotine, or a scaffold, for a crime they never committed; but not one of them has ever failed to cry: "I am innocent."

But Our Lord made no such protest, for it would have been to have falsely assumed that man is the Judge of God. Now if Our Lord, Who was Innocence, refrained from asserting His Innocence, then we who are not without sin should not forever be crying our innocence.

To do this is wrongly to admit that man, and not God, is our Judge. Our souls are to be judged not before the tribunal of men, but before the throne of the God of Love, and He "who sees in secret will reward in secret." Our eternal salvation does not depend on how the world judges us, but on how God judges us.

It matters little if our fellow citizens condemn us even when we are right, for Truth always finds its contradictors; that is why Truth is now nailed to a Cross. What does matter is that we be found right in God's judgment, for in that our eternal happiness depends. There is every chance in the world that the two judgments will differ, for man sees only the face, but God reads the heart. We can fool men, but we cannot fool God.

There was another thing Our Blessed Lord did not say to the representatives of Caesar and the Temple who sent Him to the Cross, namely, "You are unjust." The Father gave all judgment unto Him and yet He does not judge man and say: "You will suffer for this." He knew, being God as well as man, that while there is life there is hope, and His patient suffering before death might purchase the souls of many who now condemn.

Why judge them before the time for judgment? Longinus of the Roman army and Joseph of the Sanhedrin would come to His saving embrace and forgiveness even before He was taken down from the Cross. The sinner of this hour might be the saint of the next.

One reason for a long life is penance. Time is given us not just to accumulate that which we cannot take with us, but to make reparation for our sins.

That is why in the parable of the fig tree which had not borne fruit for three years and which the owner wished to cut down because it "cumbereth the ground," the dresser of the vineyard said: "Let it alone this year also, until

I dig about it, and dung it. And if happily it bear fruit" *(Luke 13:6-9)*.

So the Lord is with the wicked. He gives them another month, another year of life that they may dig their soul with penance and dung it with mortification, and happily save their souls.

If then the Lord did not judge His executioners before the hour of their judgment, why should we, who really know nothing about them anyway, judge them even when they do us wrong? While they live, may not our refraining from judgment be the very means of their conversion? In any case, judgment has not been given to us, and the world may be thankful that it has not, for God is a more merciful judge than man. "Judge not that you may not be judged" *(Matthew 7:1)*.

What Our Lord did say on the Cross was, *forgive*. Forgive your Pilates, who are too weak to defend your justice; forgive your Herods, who are too sensual to perceive your spirituality; forgive your Judases, who think worth is to be measured in terms of silver. "Forgive them — for they know not what they do."

In that sentence is packed the united love of Father and Son, whereby the holy love of God met the sin of man and remained innocent. This first word of forgiveness is the strongest evidence of Our Lord's absolute sinlessness. The rest of us at our death must witness the great parade of our sins, and the sight of them is so awful that we dare not go before God without a prayer for pardon.

Yet Jesus, on dying, craved no forgiveness, for He had no sin. The forgiveness He asked was for those who accused Him of sin. And the reason He asked for pardon was that "they know not what they do."

He is God as well as man, which means He knows all the secrets of every human heart. Because He knows all, He can find an excuse: "they know not what they do." But we know so little of our enemies' hearts, and so little of the circumstances of their acts and the good faith mingled with their evil deeds, that we are less likely to find an excuse. Because we are ignorant of their hearts, we are apt to be less excusing.

In order to judge others, we must be inside them and outside them, but only God can do this. Our neighbors are just as impenetrable to us as we are to them. Judgment on our part, then, would be wrong, for to judge without a mandate is unjust. Our Lord alone has a mandate to judge; we have not.

If possessing that mandate, and knowing all, He still found reason to forgive, then we who have no jurisdiction and who cannot possibly with our puny minds know our neighbors' hearts, have only one thing left to do; that is, to pray: "Father, forgive ... for they know not what they do."

Our Lord used the word, *forgive*, because He was innocent and knew all, but we must use it for other reasons. Firstly, because we have been forgiven greater sins by God. Secondly, because only by forgiving can hate be banished from the world. And thirdly, because our own pardon is conditioned by the pardon, we extend to others.

Firstly, we must forgive others because God has forgiven us. There is no injustice any human being has ever committed against us which is comparable to the injustice we commit against God by our sins. It is this idea Our Lord suggests in the parable of the unmerciful servant *(Matthew 18:21-35)* who was forgiven a debt of ten thousand talents by his master, and immediately afterward went out and choked a fellow-servant who owed him only a hundred pence.

The debt which the master forgave the servant was 1,250,000 times greater than the debt owed by the fellow servant. In this great disproportion is revealed how much greater are man's sins against God than are the sins of our fellowmen against us. We must, therefore, forgive our enemies because we have been forgiven the greater sin of treating God as an enemy.

And if we do not forgive the sins of our enemies, it is very likely because we have never cast up our accounts with God. Herein is to be found the secret of so much of the violence and bitterness of some men in our modern world; they refuse to think of themselves as ever having offended God and therefore never think of themselves as needing pardon.

They think they need no pardon; hence no one else should ever have it. The man who knows not his own guilt before God is apt to be most unforgiving to others, as David at the time of his worst sin.

Our condemnation is often the veil for our own weakness: we cover up our own nakedness with the mantle of criticism; we see the mote in our brother's eye, but never the beam in our own. We carry all our neighbor's faults on a sack in front of us, and all our own on a sack behind us.

The cruelest master is the man who never learned to obey, and the severest judge is the man who never examines his own conscience. The man who is conscious of his need of absolution is the one who is most likely to be indulgent to others.

Such was Paul, who, writing to Titus, finds a reason for being merciful to men: "For we ourselves also were some time unwise, incredulous, erring, slaves to divers desires and pleasures, living in malice and envy, hateful, and hating one another" *(Titus 3:3)*.

It is the forgetfulness of its own sins which makes modern hate so deep and bitter. Men throttle their neighbor for a penny because they forget God forgave them a debt of ten thousand talents. Let them only think of how good God has been to them, and they will begin to be good to others.

A second reason for forgiving those who make us suffer unjustly is that if we do not forgive, hate will multiply until the whole world is hateful. Hate is extremely fertile; it reproduces itself with amazing rapidity.

Communism knows hate can disrupt society more quickly than armies, that is why it never speaks of charity. That too is why it sows hatred in labor against capital; hatred in atheists against religion; hatred in themselves against all who oppose them.

How can all this hatred be stopped when one man is slapping another on the cheek? There is only one way, and that is by turning the other cheek, which means: "I forgive; I refuse to hate you. If I hate you, I will add my quota to the sum total of hate. This I refuse to do. I will kill your hate; I will drive it from the earth. I will love you."

That was the way Stephen conquered the hate of those who killed him; namely, by praying: "Lord, lay not this sin to their charge" *(Acts 7:59)*. He was practically repeating the first word from the Cross.

And that prayer of forgiveness won over the heart of a young man named Saul who stood nearby, holding the garments of those who stoned him, and "consenting to his death." If Stephen had cursed Saul, Saul might never have become St. Paul. What a loss that would have been! But hate lost the day because Stephen forgave.

In our day love is still winning victories over hate. When Father Pro of Mexico, a few years ago was shot by the Mexican revolutionists, he turned to them and said: "I forgive you; kneel and I will give you my blessing." And every soldier in the firing line fell on his knees for the blessing.

It was a beautiful spectacle indeed to see a man forgiving those who are about to kill him! Only the Captain refused to kneel, and it was he who did what to Father Pro was an act of great kindness — ushered him, by a blow through the heart, into the company of Stephen, a martyr of the Church of God.

During the Civil War in Spain when the Reds were slaughtering hundreds of priests, one of them was lined up before the firing squad with his arms tightly bound by ropes. Facing the firing squad, he said: "Untie these ropes and let me give you my blessing before I die." The Communists untied the ropes, but they cut off his hands. Then sarcastically they said: "All right, see if you can give us your blessing now." And the priest raised the stumps of his arms as crimson rags and with blood dripping from them like beads forming on the earth the red rosary of redemption, he moved them about in the form of a cross. Thus hate was defeated, for he refused to nourish it. Hate died as he forgave and the world has been better for it.

Finally, we must forgive others, for on no other condition will our own sins be forgiven. In fact, it is almost a moral impossibility for God to forgive us unless we in turn forgive. Has He not said: "Blessed are the merciful: for they shall obtain mercy" *(Matthew 5:7)*. "Forgive, and you shall be forgiven. Give, and it shall be given unto you . . . For with the same measure that you shall mete withal, it shall be measured to you again" *(Luke 6:37-38)*.

The law is inescapable. Unless we sow, we shall not reap; unless we show mercy to our fellowmen, God will revoke His mercy toward us. As in the parable, the master cancelled the forgiveness of the servant because he refused to show a smaller mercy to his fellowman, "so also shall my heavenly Father do to you, if you forgive not every one, his brother from your hearts" *(Matthew 18:35)*.

If a box is filled with salt it cannot be filled with sand, and if our hearts are filled with hatred of our neighbor, how can God fill them with His love? It is just as simple as that. There can be, and there will be no mercy toward us unless we ourselves are merciful. The real test of the Christian then is not how much he loves his friends, but how much he loves his enemies.

The divine command is clear: "Love your enemies: do good to them that hate you: and pray for them that persecute and calumniate you: that you may be the children of your Father who is in heaven, who maketh his sun to rise upon the good, and bad, and raineth upon the just and the unjust.

"For if you love them, that love you, what reward shall you have? Do not even the publicans this? And if you salute your brethren only, what do you more? Do not also the heathens this?" *(Matthew 5:44-47)*.

Forgive, then! Forgive even seventy times seven! Soften the pillow of death by forgiving your enemies their little sins against you, that you may be forgiven your great sins against God. Forgive those who hate you, that you may conquer them by love. Forgive those who injure you, that you may be forgiven your offenses. Our world is so full of hate!

The race of the clenched fists is multiplying like the race of Cain. The struggle for existence has become existence for struggle. There are even those who talk about peace only because they want the world to wait until they are strong enough for war.

"Dear Lord, what can we, thy followers, do to bring peace to the world? How can we stop brother rising up against brother and class against class, blurring the very sky with their cross-covered Golgothas? Thy First Word on the Cross gives the answer: We must see in the body of every man who hates, a soul that was made to love. If we are too easily offended by their hate, it is because we have forgotten either the destiny of their souls or our own sins. Forgive us our trespasses as we forgive those who trespass against us. Forgive us for ever having been offended. Then we, like Thee, may

find among our executioners another Longinus, who had forgotten there was love in a heart until he opened it with a lance."

PAIN

(The Second Word from the Cross)

*"This day thou shalt be
with me in paradise."*

THE FIRST WORD FROM the Cross tells us what should be our attitude toward unjust suffering, but the Second Word tells us what should be our attitude toward pain. There are two ways of looking at it; one is to see it without purpose, the other to see it with purpose.

The first view regards pain as opaque, like a stone wall; the other view regards it as transparent, like a window pane. The way we will react to pain depends entirely upon our philosophy of life. As the poet has put it:

"Two men looked out through their
prison bars;
The one saw mud, the other stars."

Dale Carnegie

In like manner, there are those who, looking upon a rose, would say: "Isn't it a pity that those roses have thorns"; while others would say: "Isn't it consoling that those thorns have roses!' These two attitudes are manifested in the two thieves crucified on either side of Our Blessed Lord. The thief on the right is the model for those for whom pain has a meaning; the thief on the left is the symbol of unconsecrated suffering.

Consider first the thief on the left. He suffered no more than the thief on the right, but he began and ended his crucifixion with a curse. Never for a moment did he correlate his sufferings with the Man on the central cross. Our Lord's prayer of forgiveness meant no more to that thief than the flight of a bird.

He saw no more purpose in his suffering than a fly sees purpose in the window pane that floods man's habitation with God's warmth and sunlight. Because he could not assimilate his pain and make it turn to the nourishment of his soul, pain turned against him as a foreign substance taken into the stomach turns against it and infects and poisons the whole system.

That is why he became bitter, why his mouth became like a crater of hate, and why he cursed the very Lord Who could have shepherded him into peace and paradise.

The world today is full of those who, like the thief on the left, see no meaning in pain. Knowing nothing of the Redemption of Our

Lord they are unable to fit pain into a pattern; it becomes just an odd patch on the crazy quilt of life. Life becomes so wholly unpredictable for them that "a troubled manhood follows their baffled youth."

Never having thought of God as anything more than a name, they are now unable to fit the stark realities of life into His Divine Plan. That is why so many who cease to believe in God become cynics, killing not only themselves but, in a certain sense, even the beauties of flowers and the faces of children for whom they refuse to live.

The lesson of the thief on the left is clear: Pain of itself does not make us better; it is very apt to make us worse. No man was ever better simply because he had an earache. Unspiritualized suffering does not improve man; it degenerates him. The thief at the left is no better for his crucifixion: it sears him, burns him, and tarnishes his soul.

Refusing to think of pain as related to anything else, he ends by thinking only of himself and who would take him down from the cross. So it is with those who have lost their faith in God. To them Our Lord on a cross is only an event in the history of the Roman Empire; He is not a message of hope or a proof of love.

They would not have a tool in their hands five minutes without discovering its purpose, but they live their lives without ever having inquired its meaning. Having no reason for living, suffering embitters them, poisons them, and finally, the great door of life's opportunity is closed in their faces, and like the thief on the left, they go out into the night unblessed.

Now, look at the thief on the right — the symbol of those for whom pain has a meaning. At first, he did not understand it and therefore joined in the curses with the thief on the left. But just as sometimes a flash of lightning will illumine the path we have missed, so to the Saviour's forgiveness of His executioners illumined for the thief the road of mercy.

He began to see that if pain had no reason, Jesus would not have embraced it. If the cross had no purpose, Jesus would not have climbed it. Surely He Who claimed to be God would never have taken that badge of shame unless it could be transformed and transmuted to some holy purpose.

Pain was beginning to be comprehensible to the thief; for the present at least it meant an occasion to do penance for his life of crime. And the moment that that light came to him he rebuked the thief on the left saying: "Neither dost thou fear God, seeing thou art under the same condemnation? And we indeed suffer justly, for we receive the due reward of our deeds; but this man hath done no evil" *(Luke 23:40-41).*

Now he saw pain as doing to his soul like to that which fire does to gold: burning away the dross. Or something like that which fever does to disease; killing the germs. Pain was dropping scales away from his eyes; and, turning toward the central cross, he no longer saw a crucified man, but a Heavenly King.

Surely, He Who can pray for pardon for His murderers will not cast off a thief: "Lord, remember me when Thou shalt come into Thy kingdom." Such great faith found its reward: "Amen I say to thee, this day thou shalt be with Me in paradise" *(Luke 23:42-43).*

Pain in itself is not unbearable; it is the failure to understand its meaning that is unbearable. If that thief did not see purpose in pain, he would never have saved his soul. Pain can be the death of our soul, or it can be its life.

It all depends on whether or not we link it up with Him Who, "having joy set before him, endured the cross." One of the greatest tragedies in the world is wasted pain. Pain without relation to the cross is like an unsigned check — without value. But once we have it countersigned with the Signature of the Saviour on the Cross, it takes on an infinite value.

A feverish brow that never throbs in unison with a Head crowned with thorns, or an aching hand never borne in patience with a Hand on the Cross, is sheer waste. The world is worse for that pain when it might have been so much the better.

All the sick-beds in the world, therefore, are either on the right side of the Cross or on the left; their position is determined by whether, like the thief on the left, they ask to be taken down, or, like the thief on the right, they ask to be taken up.

It is not so much what people suffer that makes the world mysterious; it is rather how much they miss when they suffer. They seem to forget that even as children they made obstacles in their games in order to have something to overcome.

Why, then, when they grow into man's estate, should there not be prizes won by effort and struggle? Cannot the spirit of man rise with adversity as the bird rises against the resistance of the wind? Do not the game fish swim upstream? Must not the alabaster box be broken to fill the house with ointment? Must not the chisel cut away the marble to bring out the form? Must not the seed falling to the ground die before it can spring forth into life? Must not the little streams speed into the ocean to escape their stagnant self-content? Must not grapes be crushed that there may be wine to drink, and wheat ground that there may be bread to eat?

Why then cannot pain be made redemption? Why under the alchemy of Divine Love cannot crosses be turned into crucifixes? Why cannot chastisements be regarded as penances? Why cannot we use a cross to become God-like? We cannot become like Him in His Power: we cannot become like Him in His Knowledge.

There is only one way we can become like Him, and that is in the way He bore His sorrows and His Cross. And that way was with love. "Greater love than this no man hath, that a man lay down his life for his friends." It is love that makes pain bearable.

As long as we feel it is doing good for another, or even for our own soul by increasing the glory of God, it is easier to bear. A mother keeps a vigil at the bedside of her sick child. The world calls it "fatigue," but she calls it love.

A little child was commanded by his mother not to walk the picket fence. He disobeyed and fell, maimed himself and was never able to walk again. Being told of his misfortune, he said to his mother: "I know I will never walk again; I know it is my own fault, but if you will go on loving me I can stand anything." So it is with our own pains.

If we can be assured that God still loves and cares, then we shall find joy even in carrying on His redemptive work — by being redeemers with a small "r" as He is Redeemer with a capital "R." Then will come to us the vision of the difference between Pain and Sacrifice. Pain is sacrifice without love. Sacrifice is pain with love.

When we understand this, then we shall have an answer for those who feel that God should have let us sin without pain:

"The cry of earth's anguish went up unto
God, —
'Lord, take away pain, —
The shadow that darkens the world Thou
hast made,
The close-coiling chain
That strangles the heart, the burden that
weighs
On the wings that would soar, —
Lord, take away pain from the world Thou
hast made
That it love Thee the more.'

"Then answered the Lord to the world He
had made,
'Shall I take away pain?
And with it, the power of the soul to
endure
Made strong by the strain?
Shall I take away pity that knits heart to
heart
And sacrifice high?
Will ye lose all your heroes who lift from
the flame
White brows to the sky?
Shall I take away love that redeems with a
price
And smiles through the loss, —
Can ye spare from the lives that would
climb unto mine
The Christ on His Cross?"

George Stewart
"God and Pain"

And now this final lesson. You and I often
ask God for many favors which are never
granted. We can imagine the thief on the right
during his life asking God for many favors, and
very especially for wealth which was probably
not granted. On the other hand, though God

does not always grant our material favors, there is one prayer He always grants.

There is a favor that you and I can ask of God this very moment if we had the courage to do it, and that favor would be granted before the day is over. That prayer, which God has never refused, and will never refuse is the prayer for suffering. Ask Him to send you a cross, and you will receive it!

But why does He not always answer our prayers for *an increase in* salary, for larger commissions, for more money? Why did He not answer the prayer of the thief on the left to be taken down from the cross, and why did He answer the prayer of the thief on the right to forgive his sins?

Because material favors draw us away from Him, but the cross always draws us to Him. And God does not want the world to have us!

He wants us Himself because He died for us!

SUFFERING OF THE INNOCENT

(The Third Word from the Cross)

"Woman, behold thy son!
(Son) Behold thy mother!"

WHY DO THE INNOCENT SUFFER? We do not mean the innocent who have suffering involuntarily thrust upon them, but rather those good souls who go out in search of suffering and are impatient until they find a cross. In other words, why should there be Carmelites, Poor Clares, Trappists, Little Sisters of the Poor, and dozens of penitential orders of the Church, who do nothing but sacrifice and suffer for the sins of men?

Certainly not because suffering is necessarily connected with personal sin. Our Lord told us that much, when to those who asked concerning a blind boy, "Who hath sinned, this man, or his parents . . . ?", Our Lord answered "Neither."

If we are to find the answer, we must go not merely to the suffering of innocent people, but to the suffering of Innocence itself. In this

Third Word, our attention is riveted upon the two most sinless creatures who ever trod our sinful earth: Jesus and Mary.

Jesus Himself was sinless by nature, for He is the all holy Son of God. Mary was sinless by grace, for she is "our tainted nature's solitary boast." And yet both suffer in the extreme. Why did He suffer Who had the power of God to escape the Cross? Why did she suffer who could have dispensed herself because of her virtue, or could have been excused by her Divine Son?

Love is the key to the mystery. Love by its very nature is not selfish, but generous. It seeks not its own, but the good of others. The measure of love is not the pleasure it gives — that is the way the world judges it — but the joy and peace it can purchase for others.

It counts not the wine it drinks, but the wine it serves. Love is not a circle circumscribed by self; it is a cross with arms embracing all humanity. It thinks not of having, but of being had, not of possessing but of being possessed, not of owning but of being owned.

Love than by its nature is social. Its greatest happiness is to gird its loins and serve at the banquet of life. Its greatest unhappiness is to be denied the joy of sacrifice for others. *That is why in the face of pain, love seeks to unburden the sufferer and take his pain, and that is why in the face of sin, love seeks to atone for the injustice of him who sinned.*

Because mothers love, do they not want to take the pain of their children's wounds? Because fathers love, do they not take over the debts of wayward sons to expiate their foolishness?

What does all this mean but the "otherness" of love? In fact, love is so social it would reject emancipation from pain if the emancipation were for itself alone. Love refuses to accept individual salvation; it never bends over man, as the healthy over the sick, but enters into him to take his very sickness.

It refuses to have its eyes clear when other eyes are bedewed with tears; it cannot be happy unless everyone is happy, or unless justice is served; it shrinks from isolation and aloofness from the burdens and hungers of others. It spurns insulation from the shock of the world's sorrow, but insinuates itself into them, as if the sorrow were it's very own.

This is not difficult to understand. Would you want to be the only person in all the world who had eyes to see? Would you want to be the only one who could walk in a universe of the lame? Would you, if you loved your family, stand on the dock and watch them all drown before your very eyes?

And if not, why not? Very simply, because you love them because you feel so much one with them that their heartaches are your own heartbreaks.

Now apply this to Our Lord and His Blessed Mother. Here is love at its peak, and innocence at its best.

Can they be indifferent to that which is a greater evil than pain, namely sin? Can they watch humanity carry a cross to the Golgotha of death, while they themselves refuse to share its weight? Can they be indifferent to the outcome of love if they themselves *are* Love? If love means identification and sympathy with the one loved, then why should not God so love the world as to send His only begotten Son into it to redeem the world? And if that Divine Son loved the world enough to die for it, why should not the Mother of Love Incarnate share that redemption? If human love identifies itself with the pain of the one loved, why should not Divine Love suffer when it comes in contact with sin in man? If mothers suffer in their children if a husband grieves in the sorrow of his wife, and if friends feel the agony of their beloved's cross, why should not Jesus and Mary suffer in the humanity they love?

If you would die for your family of which you are the head, why should not He die for humanity of which He is the Head? And if the deeper the love, the more poignant the pain, why should not the Crucifixion be born of that Love?

If a sensitive nerve is touched it registers pain in the brain; and since Our Lord is the Head of suffering humanity, He felt every sin of every man as His own. That is why the Cross was inevitable.

He could not love us perfectly unless He died for us. And His Mother could not love Him perfectly unless she shared that death. That is why His life was given for us, and her heart broken for us; and that, too, is why He is Redeemer, and she is Redemptrix — because they love.

In order more completely to reveal that a Cross was made up of the juncture of Love and sin, Our Lord spoke His *Third Word* to His Mother: "Woman, behold thy son"! He did not call her 'Mother' but 'Woman'; except when addressing John the next moment He added: "[Son] Behold thy Mother."

The term 'Woman' indicated a wider relationship to all humanity than 'Mother.' It meant that she was to be not only His Mother but that she was also to be the Mother of all men, as He was the Saviour of all men. She was now to have many children — not according to the flesh, but according to the spirit. Jesus was her first-born of the flesh in joy; John was her second-born of the spirit in sorrow, and we her millionth and millionth born.

If she loved Him Who died for all men, then she must love those for whom He died. That was His clear, unmistakable meaning. The love of neighbor is inseparable from the love of God. His love had no limits; He died for every man. Her love then must have no limits.

It must not be merely unselfish; it must even be social. She must be the Mother of every man. An earthly mother loves her own children most, but Jesus is now telling her that even John is her son, too, and John was the symbol of all of us.

The Father did not spare His Son, nor did the Son spare His Mother, for love knows no bounds. Jesus had a sense of responsibility for every soul in the world; Mary, too, inspired by His love, had a corresponding sense of responsibility. If He would be the Redeemer of the wayward children, she must be their Mother.

Now does that throw any light on the problem? Why do innocent, pure, good souls leave the world and its pleasures, feast on fasts, embrace the cross, and pray their hearts out? The answer is *because they love.* "Greater love than this no man hath, that a man lay down his life for his friends."

They love the world so much that they want to save it, and they know there is no other way to save it than to die for it. Many of us so love the world that we live *in* it and are *of* it, but in the end, do nothing *for* it. Wrong indeed are they who say these innocent victims hate the world.

As soon as the world hears of a beautiful young woman or an upright young man entering the religious life, it asks: "Why did they leave the world?" They left the world, not because they hated the world, but because they loved it. They love the world with its human souls so much that they want to do all they can for it; and they can do nothing better for it than to pray that souls may one day find their way back to God.

Our Lord did not hate the world; it hated Him. But He loved it. Neither do they hate the world; they are in love with it and everyone in it. They so much love the sinners in it, that they expiate for their sins; they so much love the Communists in it, that they bless them as they send them to their God; they so much love the atheists in it, that they are willing to surrender the joy of the divine presence that the atheist may feel less afraid in the dark.

They are so much lovers of the world that they may be said to be organic with it. They know that things and souls are so much interrelated that the good which one does has repercussion on the millions, just as ten just men could have saved Sodom and Gomorrah. If a stone is thrown into the sea, it causes a ripple which widens in ever greater circles until it affects even the most distant shore; a rattle dropped from a baby's crib affects even the most distant star; a finger is burnt, and the whole body feels the pain.

The cosmos then is organic, but so also is humanity. We are all called to be members of a great family.

God is Our Father, Who sent His Son into the world to be Our Brother, and He on the Cross asked Mary to be Our Mother. Now if in the human body it is possible to graft skin from one member to another, why is it not possible also to graft prayer?

If it is possible to transfuse blood, why is it not possible also to transfuse sacrifice? Why cannot the innocent atone for the sinful?

Why cannot the real lovers of souls, who refuse to be emancipated from sorrow, do for the world what Jesus did on the cross and Mary did beneath it? The answer to this question has filled the cloisters.

No one on earth can measure the good these divine lovers are doing for the world. How often have they stayed the wrath of a righteous God! How many sinners have they brought to the confessional! How many deathbed conversions have they effected! How many persecutions have they averted!

We do not know, and they do not want to know, so long as love wins over hate. But let us not be foolish and ask: What good do they do for the world? We might as well ask: What good did the Cross do?

After all, only the innocent can understand what sin is. No one until the time of Our Lord ever thought of giving his life to save sinners, simply because no one was sinless enough to know its horrors.

We who have familiarized ourselves with it, become used to it, as a leprous patient after many years of suffering cannot wholly appreciate the evil of leprosy.

Sin has lost its horror; we never think of correlating it to the cross: we never advert to its repercussions on humanity.

"Vice is a monster of so frightful mien,
As to be hated, needs but to be seen;
Yet seen too oft, familiar with her face,
We first endure, then pity, then embrace."

Alexander Pope

The best way to know sin is by not sinning. But Jesus and Mary were wholly innocent — He by nature, she by grace; therefore, they could understand and know the evil of sin.

Having never compromised with it, there were now no compromises to be made. It was something so awful that to avoid it or to atone for it; they shrink not even from a death on the cross.

But by a peculiar paradox, though innocence hates sin, because it alone knows its gravity, it nevertheless loves the sinner. Jesus loved Peter who fell three times, and Mary chose as her companion at the foot of the cross, a converted prostitute.

What must the scandal mongers have said of that friendship as they watched Mary and Magdalen ascend and descend the hill of Calvary! But Mary braved it all, in order that in a future generation you and I might have hope in her as the "Refuge of sinners." Let there be no fear that she cannot understand our sinful misery because she is Immaculate, for if she had Magdalen as a companion then, why can she not have us now?

Dear Mother Immaculate, but seldom in history have the innocent suffered as they do today. Countless Marys and Johns stand beneath the cross guilty of no other crime than that they love the Man on the Cross. If there be no remission of sins without the shedding of blood, then let these innocent victims of hate in Russia, in Spain, and in Mexico, be the redemption of those who hate. We ask not that the hateful perish; we only ask that the sufferings of the just be the salvation of the wicked.

Thou didst suffer innocently because thou didst love us in union with thy Divine Son. Thus were we taught, that only those who cease to love ever flee from the Cross. The innocents who are slaughtered today are not the babes of Bethlehem; they are the grown-up children of Bethlehem's God — men and women who save the Church today as Bethlehem's babes once saved Jesus.

Be thou their consolation, their joy, their Mother, O Innocent Woman who binds the sons of men to the Son of God in the unity of the Father and the Holy Ghost, world without end. Amen.

GOD AND THE SOUL

(The Fourth Word from the Cross)

"My God! My God!
Why hast thou abandoned me?"

THE FIRST THREE *WORDS* on the cross have reference to physical suffering: this *Fourth Word* has reference to moral suffering or sin. Physical suffering is pain; moral suffering is evil or sin.

Our world takes sin very lightly, regarding it too often as a relic of ages, which were ignorant of evolution and psychoanalysis. It is the contrary which is true: the more we know about death and its causes the more we know about sin, for in the language of Sacred Scripture, "the wages of sin is death."

Death and sin are identified and rightly so: death in the physical order corresponds to evil in the moral order. Death in the physical order is normally the domination of a lower order over a higher order.

For example, animals and men generally die through the slow oxidation and burning out of the organism. At that moment, when the oxidation of chemical order dominates the biological order, the phenomenon called death ensues.

Now man has not only a body but also a soul. At that precise point, then, when the lower law of self-dominates the higher law of charity, when the flesh dominates the spirit, when the love of earth gains supremacy over the love of God, there is the subversion of due order, and that domination of the lower over, the higher order we call sin.

What death is to the body, that sin is to the soul, namely the surrender of life — human in one case, divine in the other. That is why St. Paul calls sin a crucifixion or the killing of the Divine Life within us: "Crucifying again to themselves the Son of God and making Him a mockery" *(Hebrews 6:6)*.

Since sin is the taking of Divine Life, it follows that nowhere else was sin better revealed than on Calvary, for there, sinful humanity crucified the Son of God in the flesh. Here sin comes to a burning focus. It manifests itself in its essence: the taking of Divine Life.

Moral evil reaches its greatest power in the taking of the life of the Man of Sorrows, for a world capable of killing the God-man is capable of doing anything.

Nothing else it can ever do will be worse, and all that it will ever do will be but the reenactment of this tragedy. There, where character was perfect, and suffering most undeserved, the victory of evil was most complete.

If sin could have found a reason for being hateful towards God, the crime would have been less heinous. But His enemies could find no fault in Him except His all-compassing Goodness.

But goodness is the one thing sin cannot endure, for goodness is sin's constant reproach. The wicked always hate the good. The very unreasonableness of the judgment against Our Lord — for even Pilate admitted he found the Man innocent — was the mirror of the anarchy of sin.

Sin chose the battleground, set up the gallows of torture, influenced the judges, inflamed the crowds, and decided on the death of Divine Life.

It could have chosen no better way of revealing its nature. It refused to have God on earth, and so it lifted His Cross above the earth.

Sin wanted no shepherding calls to repentance, and so it fastened Him to a tree. "He came unto his own, and his own received him not." They abandoned Him at birth: they would now abandon Him in death. Thus would sin reach its most perfect expression: *for sin is the abandonment of God by man.*

But the Saviour is on the Cross not to go down to defeat but to redeem from sin. How better can He atone for sin than by taking upon Himself one of its most bitter consequences?

Since sin is the abandonment of God by man, He now wills to feel its consequence: the abandonment of man by God. Such is the meaning of the *Fourth Word* uttered in the moment when darkness crept over Calvary like a leprosy: "My God, my God, why hast thou abandoned Me?"

Man rejected God. Our Lord willed to feel that rejection within Himself. Man turned away from God; He, Who is God united hypostatically with a human nature, now wills to feel that awful wrench, as if He Himself were guilty. It was all deliberate. He was laying His life down of Himself, even when they thought they were taking it away.

He willed to be identified with man, and now He resolves to travel the road to the end and to take upon Himself the terrible loneliness of sin. His pain of abandonment expressed in this *Fourth Word* was double: the abandonment by man and God.

Man abandons Him because He refuses to deny His Divinity; God seemingly abandons

Him because He wills to forego divine consolation, to taste the bitter dregs of sin that the cup of sin may be emptied.

As a symbol of that double abandonment by heaven and earth, His cross is suspended between both, and yet uniting them for the first time since Adam abandoned God.

None of us knows the deeper meaning of the cry; no one can know. He alone Who is sinless can know the utter horror of sin which caused it.

But this we do know, that at this moment He permitted Himself to feel the solitariness and abandonment caused by sin. And yet His cry proves that though men do abandon Him, they never completely desert Him, for a man can no more shake off God than he can deny parentage.

That is why His cry of abandonment was prefaced with the cry of belief: "My God, my God!" Into it was concentrated the loneliness of every sinful heart that ever lived.

And yet with it, all was the divine nostalgia — the loneliness of the atheist who says there is no God and yet under starry skies believes in His Power.

So, too, the loneliness of fallen away Catholics, who have left the Church not for reasons but for things and who, like prodigal children, still dream of the happiness of the servants in the Father's house.

So, too, the loneliness of the enemies of religion who testify to its reality by the bitterness of their hate, for no man hates a mirage.

So, too, the loneliness of the pessimists who complain against the evil in the world, but only because they believe more deeply still in the reality of Justice.

So, too, the loneliness of sinners who hate themselves for hating virtue.

So, too, the loneliness of the worldly who live without religion, not because they deny it, but because they are "sore adread lest, having Him, [they] should have nought beside."

All in their own way are saying: "I abandon and yet I believe."

It is just that which makes one wonder if there is really any sinner who has ever gone so far down its dark, damp corridors as to forget that he left the light. The words on the Cross seem to say so much.

Not even those direct descendants of the executioners who pillage churches and crucify Christ's ambassadors have yet proved it, for how can one hate so intensely that which he believes to be only a dream?

If religion is the opium of the people, why, instead of putting men to sleep, does it awaken them to martyrdom? There is no explanation; only the Infinite can be infinitely hated and infinitely loved.

That is why sinners crucified Our Lord, and why the crucifixion made saints. Our Lord is the Infinite God.

It is hard for us to grasp the awfulness of sin, but if we cannot see it in its relation to the death of the all holy One of God, then we are beyond repentance.

The truth is that as long as sin endures, the Crucifixion endures. Clovis, the King of the Franks, on hearing for the first time the story of the Crucifixion said: "If I had been there with my army, this never would have happened." But the fact is, Clovis was there. So was his army. So were we.

The Crucifixion atoned not only for the sins of the past but also for the sins of the future.

"I saw the Son of God go by
Crowned with a crown of thorns.
'Was it not finished, Lord,' said I.
'And all the anguish borne?'

"He turned on me His awful eyes,
'Hast thou not understood?
Lo, every soul is a Calvary
And every sin a rood!' "

Rachael A. Taylor

Because our body seems closer to us than our soul, we are apt to think of pain as being a greater evil than sin. But such is not the case: "Fear ye not them that kill the body . . . but rather fear him that can destroy both soul and body in hell."

Thus the reality of sin in the Crucifixion and the idea of Hell became related. The Cross proves that life is fraught with tremendous issues; that sin is so terrible that full payment in justice could be made only by the death of God-made-man.

If sin cost the death of Divine Life, then the refusal to accept Redemption can mean nothing less than eternal death or Hell.

Life then is not a mere experience; it is a drama which involves issues of Eternal Life and Eternal Death. Those who would rob Justice of hell would rob Christ of His Cross.

Were we but animals, our choices would pass away with their fulfillment, but just as our thoughts are fastened to Truth, which is unchangeable, so, too, our resolves are registered on the scroll of Perfect Goodness, which is eternal.

If in our business we take from our cash registers the slip on which is recorded the debits and credits of the day, shall we be so unreasonable as to believe that we, who live by such an order, should ourselves be governed any differently?

Why then at the end of our day's work on earth, should not the Divine Bookkeeper find registered on our consciences our answer to the question of whether our life has been a failure or a success? Either we lose our soul or we find it; either we live or we die.

And if such a fate does not come at the end of our story, then the Cross is a mockery and life is vain. But seeing how high we can rise, and how low we can fall, we can see the importance of our choices — the danger of being careless and the thrill of being brave.

As one writer has put it, "They are cowards who educate us to think that we are meant to stop at home in swaddling clothes, protected from fresh air and all possible dangers. They would make us soft and effeminate and unfit for the hurly-burly of life. This is no man's life but a tame travesty of it. All that is best in us revolts against coddling and the denial of all risk and adventure. What we need is some summons to the semi-divine courage which is latent in all of us, some challenge to risk all that we have for love. Imagine a man born of woman, ambling along on some old nag or wrapped up in some limousine to conquer the earth and to conquer himself and to make himself fit for the Divine Eros. I am tired of this cheapening of stupendous issues; I demand that Hell be given back to the world." (M. C. D'Arcy, S. J., The Pain of This World, p. 129.)

And if it be not given back to the world, then men will say, no matter how foul we become, all will be well with us in the end.

But as long as Hell remains, we have a standard by which evil can be judged, by which those who trample the love of man and God under foot can be measured, by which those who attempt to drive God from the earth He made, can be weighed.

If a man wants to know his worth, let him take one look at the Man on the Cross. There Love stands Crucified! If he crucified Love, then he is without Love; and to be without Love is Hell!

If he crucifies his lower self to be Christ like, then he is in love, and to be in love with Love is heaven.

Dear Saviour, open our eyes to see that our forgetfulness of the horror of sin is the beginning of our ruin. Too prone are we to blame finances, economics, and balances of trade for our ills, our woes; too unmindful are we that these are but the symptoms of our rebellion against Thy Divine Law.

Because we have rebelled against Thee, our Creator, creatures have turned against one another, and the world becomes one vast charnel house of hate and envy.

Give us light to see, O Lord, that it was sin which hardened itself into Thy nails, wove itself into Thy thorns, and congealed itself into Thy Cross.

But let us also see that if Thou didst take the Cross for us, then we must be worth saving; for if the Cross is the measure of our sin, then the crucifix is the pledge of our redemption, through the same Christ Our Lord. Amen.

THE NEED OF ZEAL
(The Fifth Word from the Cross)

"I thirst."

THE FOURTH WORD is the *suffering of the soul* without God; the *Fifth Word* is the suffering of God without the soul. The cry, "I thirst," refers not to physical thirst.

It was His soul that was burning and His Heart that was on fire. He was thirsting for the souls of men. The Shepherd was lonely without His sheep; the Creator was yearning for His creatures; the First-born was looking for His brethren.

All during His life, He had been searching for souls. He left heaven to find them among the thorns; it mattered little if they made a crown of them for Him, so long as He could find the one that was lost.

He said He came "not to call the just, but sinners," and His Heart thirsted for them now more than ever. He could not be happy until every sheep, and every lamb was in His sheepfold. "Other sheep I have, that are not of this fold: them also I must bring . . . and there shall be one fold and one shepherd."

There was sorrow in His sad complaint during life; "You will not come to me"; but there is tragedy in the last cry: "I thirst."

There was probably no moment during the three hours of redemption in which Our Lord suffered more than in this. Pains of the body are nothing compared to the agonies of the soul.

Taking His life did not mean so much to Him, for He was really laying it down of Himself. But for man to spurn His Love — that was enough to break His Heart.

It is difficult for us to grasp the intensity of this suffering, simply because none of us ever loves enough. We have not the capacity for love that He has. Therefore we can never miss so much when it is denied.

But when our tiny little hearts are sometimes denied the love they crave, we do get some faint inkling of what must have gone on in His Own Great Heart.

The faithful loyal wife whose husband is snatched from her by death, the mother whose son refuses to visit her and bless her declining days with filial affection, the friend who has sacrificed all only to be betrayed by one for whom he gave all — all these experience the keenest and bitterest of all human sufferings:

the pangs of unrequited love. Such victims can and really do die of a broken heart.

But what is this love for another human being, compared to the love of God for man? The affection a human heart bears for another lessens as it multiplies the objects of its love, just as a river loses its fullness the more it divides itself into little streams.

But with God, there is no decrease of love with the increase of objects loved, any more than a voice loses its strength because a thousand ears hear it.

Each human heart can break His Sacred Heart all over again; each soul has within itself the potentiality of another crucifixion. No one can love as much as Our Lord; no one, therefore, can suffer as much.

Added to this was the fact that His infinite Mind saw within that second, all the unfaithful hearts that would ever live until the end of time; all who would follow like Judas, and then betray; all who would fall and refuse His helping Hand; in a word, all who would pass by His Cross and only stop, with the executioners to shake dice for His garments, while within a stone's throw of them would be the Prize so precious it was worth gambling their very lives away.

It was this picture of ungrateful men, which renewed the Agony of the Garden and caused His Death. He died of thirst in the desert of human hearts!

From this Word, we discover this great lesson: the necessity of our loving our fellow men as Our Lord loves us.

If Jesus Christ thirsted for souls, must not a Christian also thirst? If He came to cast fire upon the earth, must not a Christian be enkindled? If He came to bring us the seed of Life, must not that seed fructify and bear fruit? If He lit a Light in our minds, must we not be illumined? Has He not called us to be His Apostles and His Ambassadors, in order that His Incarnation might be prolonged through the continued dispensation of the divine through the human?

A Christian then is a man to whom Our Lord has given other men. He breaks bread to the poor through our hands, He consoles the sick through our lips, He visits the sorrowful upon our feet, He sees the fields of harvest through our eyes, and He gathers the bundles into His everlasting barns through our toil.

To be worthy of the name Christian, then, means that we too, must thirst for the spread of the Divine Love; and if we do not thirst, then we shall never be invited to sit down at the banquet of Life.

Crowns shall be given only to the victors, and the chalice of everlasting wine only to those who thirst.

A Catholic who does not strive to spread his Faith is a parasite on the Life of the Church; he who is not girding his loins for apostolate is abdicating his seat on the dais of Christianity; he who is not bearing fruit is like a tree cut down on the road impeding the march of the army of God. He who is not a conquering spirit is a renegade.

The torch of Faith has been given to us not to delight our eyes but to enkindle the torches of our fellow men. Unless we burn and are on fire for the Divine Cause a glacial invasion will sweep the earth which will be the end, for "The Son of man, when he cometh, shall he find, think you, faith on earth?"

The measure of our apostolate is the intensity of our love. A human heart loves to talk about the object of his love and loves to hear that object praised.

If we love Our Lord, then we will love to talk about His Holy Cause, for "out of the abundance of the heart the mouth speaketh." To those who have such love, there is never the excuse of a want of opportunity.

Our Lord has told us "the harvest indeed is great, but the laborers are few."

To the zealous Christian every country is a mission country; every banquet room a Simon's house where another Magdalen can be found; every ship another bark of Peter from which nets of salvation can be let down; every crowded city street another Tyre and Sidon where the whelps that eat the crumbs from the master's table can be rewarded for their faith; and every cross is a throne where thieves become courtiers.

There are those that would destroy every mark of the Saviour's feet from the face of the earth. There are those who would renew the Crucifixion by hating those who preach His love; the wicked today hide not the shame of their sins but seek to find others and make others like unto themselves, in order to find consolation in their corporate decadence.

But these are not reason why Christians should go into the catacombs and leave the earth to the race of Cain. While these enemies of Divine Love live, they are still purchasable by Divine Grace and are potential children of the Kingdom of God. They are our opportunities.

Our Lord thirsted for them on the Cross, and we must thirst for them too, and love them enough to try to save them.

One thing is certain; we are not called to be Christians to damn them but to save them, in order that all men may be one great redeemed humanity and Christ its Sacred Heart.

Some will always resist, but there are no hopeless cases. Sometime ago in Spain, two hundred men were ordered shot when the Spanish people won over a city from the forces of anarchy.

These two hundred men had burned churches, murdered priests and nuns, ravaged virgins, and were now to expiate their crimes. The Carmelites who had suffered from their hands began a novena of prayer and fasting that they might be converted to God before their death. Out of the two hundred, one hundred and ninety-eight at the end of the novena received the Sacraments and died in peace with their Saviour.

Something we must never forget is that every man wants to be happy, but he cannot be happy without God. Below the surface of every heart, down deep in its secret gardens, is a craving for that for which it was made, as even the caged bird still retains its love of flying.

As the Holy Father put it: "Beneath the ashes of these perverted lives there are to be found sparks which can be fanned into a flame." Even those who hate religion have never really lost it; if they had, they would not hate it so much.

The intensity of their hate is the proof of the reality of that which they hate. If they really lost religion, they would not spend all their energy attempting to make everyone else lose theirs; a man who has lost a watch does not go about persuading others to lose their watches.

Thus hate is but their vain attempt to despise. That is why we are not to consider them beyond evangelization.

They can still be brought back even at the last moment, as the thief, or as Arthur Rimbaud. Here was a man who blasphemed Christ intensely in this life by his writings; a man whose greatest thrill was to intoxicate anyone who spoke to him of God and Our Lady, in order to berate and even physically abuse him.

He even delighted in breaking his mother's heart to whom he wrote: "Happily this life is the only one; which is obvious because one cannot imagine another life with more boredom in it than this one."

Then came his end, which is described for us in the language of François Mauriac: "Now imagine a human being who has great powers of resistance, who is much more masterful than I am, and who hates this servitude.

"Imagine a nature irritated and exasperated to distraction by this mysterious servitude and finally delivered over to an abandoned hatred of the cross.

"He spits on this sign which he drags after him and assures himself that the bonds which attach him to it could never stand out against a methodical and planned degradation of his soul and spirit.

"Thus he cultivates blasphemy and perfects it as an art and fortifies his hatred of sacred things with an armor of scornful contempt.

"Then suddenly, above this stupendous defilement, a voice rises, complainingly, appealingly; it is hardly so much as a cry, and no sooner has the sky received it than the echo is smothered by frightful jeers and by the laugh of the devil.

"As long as this man is strong enough, he will drag this cross as a prisoner his ball-chain, never accepting it. He will obstinately insist on wearing this wood along all the paths of the world. He will choose the lands of fire and ashes most suited to consume it.

"However heavy the cross becomes, it will not exhaust his hatred until the fateful day, the turning-point in his destiny when he sinks down at last under the weight of the tree and under its agonizing embrace.

"He still writhes, pulls himself together and then sinks down again, hurling out a last blasphemy. From his hospital bed, he brings abominable accusations against the nuns who are tending him; he treats the angelic sister as a fool and an idiot, and then, at last, he breaks off. This is the moment marked from all eternity.

"The cross which has dragged him for thirty-seven years and which he has denied and covered with spittle offers its arms to him: the dying man throws himself upon it, presses it to him, clings to it, embraces; he is serenely sad, and heaven is in his eyes. His voice is heard: 'Everything must be prepared in my room, everything must be arranged. The chaplain will come back with the Sacraments. You will see. They're going to bring the candles and the lace. There must be white linen everywhere. . . .' "

No! Religion is not the opium of the people. Opium is the drug of deserters who are afraid to face the Cross — the opiate that gives momentary escape from the Hound of Heaven in pursuit of the human soul.

Religion, on the contrary, is the elixir which spurs a soul on to the infinite goal for which it was made. Religion supplies the profoundest desires.

The greatest thirst of all is the thirst of unrequited love — the hand reached out which never grasps; the arms outstretched which never embrace the hand knocking on a door which is never opened. It is these things religion satisfies by making man think less about his passing desires and more about his ultimate desire.

His passing desires are multiple and fleeting — gold one minute, food another, pleasure another. But his ultimate desire is unique and abiding — the perfect happiness of everlasting joy and peace. It is our duty to lead men to the realization of this desire.

Those who hate religion are seeking religion; those who wrongly condemn are still seeking justice; those who overthrow order are seeking a new order; even those who blaspheme are adoring their own gods — but still adoring.

From certain points of view, they are all prisoners of Divine Love; they are confusing desires with *the* desire, passions with love.

They are all living in the shadow of the Cross, they are all thirsting for the Fountain of Divine Life. Their lips were made to drink — and we must not refuse to reach them the cup.

A PLANNED UNIVERSE

(The Sixth Word from the Cross)

"It is finished."

IN THE FACE OF THE UNDESERVED suffering of the just, the unmerited prosperity of the wicked, the misery of the merciful, the pleasures of the sinful, many will ask this question: Is this a planned universe, or is it the plaything of chance?

This question would have been unanswerable in this life had not Goodness itself descended into the level of the world's woe, deliberately and willfully. But once the Best freely goes down to the worst, and fits it into His plan and purpose, then no man can ever be without hope.

If a man who knows nothing about electricity is told that a bolt of electricity more powerful than lightning is to be released by a scientist in a small laboratory, that man will not fear the result, so long as he is certain that the scientist knows what he is doing.

He reasons that the scientist understands the nature of electricity, even though he does not. If the scientist hurls that otherwise destructive fire in a tiny room, it must be because he knows how to control its force. In other words, he has a plan or purpose.

In like manner, if God, Who could have foregone the trials and sorrows of man, and yet by a free act descends to man, assumes his nature, and unites it with His Own Divine Nature, and then with eyes open and with full knowledge of the world's iniquity, walks into it and even embraces it, it must be because it fits into His Divine pattern.

Our Blessed Lord did not walk blindly into a world capable of crucifying virtue, as you and I might walk into an unknown forest. He came into it as a doctor into his hospital, with full knowledge of how to deal with pain.

His whole course was charted beforehand; nothing took Him by surprise. At any given moment He had the Power to overcome. But He would not use the Power regardless of how much He was challenged until He *willed* it.

It is this Divine Knowledge which explains His rejoinder to Mary and Joseph in the temple when He was only twelve years of age: "Did you not know that I must be about my Father's business?" Already He talks of a plan, and in particular of a plan that is made in Heaven.

It also explains His many prophecies concerning His death, its time, its place, and its circumstances, and the almost impatient urge He had to realize it. "I have a baptism wherewith I am to be baptized: and how I am straitened until it be accomplished!"

Death then would not be a stumbling block to Him as it was to Socrates, for whom it was but an unwanted interruption of his teaching. For Our Lord, death was the goal He was seeking, the supreme objective of His mission on earth.

Everyone else who ever came into the world, came into it to live. Our Lord came into it to *die*. But that death with its scourgings and tears would not come to Him in an unguarded moment.

Many times during His life when His enemies sought to kill Him, He said His "hour was not yet come." When "the hour" He set did come, He refused the help of heaven and earth to postpone it or escape it.

He refused heaven's help, for had He not said: "Thinkest thou that I cannot ask my Father, and he will give me presently more than twelve legions of angels?" He refused earth's help, for He told Peter: "Put up thy sword into the scabbard." His enemies did not come to Him: He went to them. And He went saying:

"This is your hour, your hour of darkness. Your hour when I allow you to do with Me whatever you please; the hour when I might turn my back upon the ills of humanity, but in which I drink its chalice of bitterness even to its very dregs." He "Having joy set before him, endured the cross."

Bodily suffering, mental anguish, bitter disappointment, the false judgment of justice, the betrayal of true friendship, the court's perversion of honesty, and the violent separation from a mother's love — all these He took upon Himself knowingly, freely, deliberately, and purposely.

Then after three hours of crucifixion, surveying all the prophecies made about Him in Old Testament days, and the prophecies He had made of Himself, and seeing them all fulfilled and the last stitch drawn on the tapestry of His Life and the pattern completed, He uttered His sixth word — a word of triumph: "It is finished."

That cry meant: This is a planned universe. Suffering fits into it. Otherwise He would have refused it. The cross fits into it. Otherwise He would not have embraced it. The crown of thorns fits into it. Otherwise He would not have worn it.

Nothing was accidental; everything was ordered. His Father's business was completed. The plan was finished.

The full significance of the plan was not revealed until three days later when the Seed, which fell to the ground, arose into the newness of Life. It was this plan Our Lord gave to the disciple at Emmaus: "Ought not Christ to have suffered these things and so to enter into his glory?"

In other words, unless there is a Good Friday in our lives, there will never be an Easter Sunday; unless we die to this world, we shall not live in the next unless there is the crown of thorns, there will never be the halo of light; unless there is the cross, there will never be an empty tomb; unless we lose our life, we shall not find it; unless we are crucified with Christ, we shall never rise with Christ.

Such is the plan, and on our choice depends eternal issues. Our attitude toward the inescapable cross immortalizes us, either for gain or loss.

And though the plan seems hard, it is not blind, for Our Lord has not merely told us to follow Him — He has led the way. We can follow His footsteps out of the dark forest of our sufferings, but we can never say: He does not know what it means to suffer.

He suffered first to teach us how to bear it. He did not say: "Go to the Cross," but He did say: "Come, follow Me." Because He was God, He knew that men would not go just because they were told, but that they would follow if an example were given.

Our Lord made use of the contradictions of life to redeem us; we must make use of the same contradictions to apply the fruits of that redemption. His plan is finished for He is now enjoying glory. Our plan is not yet finished, for we have not yet saved our souls.

But everything we do must be directed to that one supreme goal, for "what doth it profit a man, if he gain the whole world, and suffer the loss of his own soul." Is not that the reason why, in God's plan of the universe, suffering generally comes at the end instead of at the beginning? This is a fact.

Youth is full of hopes; age is burdened with cares. Paradise came at the beginning of human history, and seven vials of wrath will come at its end. The angels sang at His birth, but His executioners blasphemed at His death.

Even in religion, the greatest spiritual joys seem to come at ordination, or at reception of the veil, or at conversion, or at the marriage ceremony.

Later on, God seems to withdraw His consoling sweetness, as a mother no longer coaxes a grown child with candy, in order to teach us that we must walk on our own feet, and work for the joys beyond.

As reasonable beings, we must ask why suffering, sadness, disillusionment, and cares, all seem to come in the evening of life?

The first reason seems to be to remind us that earth is not a paradise and that the life, truth, and love we crave, is not to be found here below.

As Abraham was told to go out of his country, so we seem to be told by life's bitterness to go out of ourselves, to look beyond and upwards to the completion of our task.

It is the burn of the fire that makes the child snatch his hand away, and it is the burden and bitterness of life that makes us draw ourselves away from earth. God is, as it were, urging us on to finish our lives and not merely to have them end, as the animals that rise to eat and then lie down to die.

Then, too, God permits these crosses in the twilight of our lives in order to supply the defects of our love. If we gave our young bones to the world, our sufferings remind us that we can still give our dry bones to God.

The crucifixion gave the good thief his one good opportunity for making amends for his failure to love and enabled him by an act of love to purchase Paradise that very day.

Too many of us are like St. Augustine, who during the delirious viciousness of early life, said: "I want to be good, a little later on, dear Lord, but not now."

It takes a cross to jolt us back again into the plan, just as many mechanical devices are restored to order by a jolt. Life's wrenches and throbs do more than anything else to convince us that we can never find happiness on earth; and if happiness could be found here, man would never so universally have sought God.

"If there had anywhere appeared in space
Another place of refuge, where to flee
Our hearts had taken refuge in that place,
And not with Thee.

"For we against creation's bars had beat
Like prisoner eagles, through great
worlds had sought
Though but a foot of ground to plant our
feet
Where Thou wert not.

"And only when we found in earth and air
In Heaven or hell, that such might
nowhere be
That we could not flee from Thee
anywhere
We fled to Thee."

Richard Trench

This Sixth Word explains that really astounding fact that we have in this life greater capacities for pain than for pleasure.

We can enjoy pleasures, but if we continue in them abnormally, they reach a point where they turn into pain. They do not lead us on and on to richer Elysian fields; rather do they turn back on us and wound us. Even the very repetition of a pleasure dulls the pleasure itself. Tickling begins with laughter and ends with pain.

But with pain it is different. In moments of intense suffering, we feel we could not bear it if it continued a minute longer. It goes on beyond that minute, and yet we tap new layers of endurability. But never does pain pass into pleasure. No toothache ever becomes fun just because it lasts a week.

Now, why is it that we have greater resources for pain than for pleasure? The real reason is this: if we live our lives as God intended that we should, then we should leave pain behind in this world and enjoy everlasting bliss in the next. Pleasure is reserved for the next world; that is why it plays traitor to us here. Pain is not intended for the next world; that is why we can exhaust it here. Pain exists in the next world only for those who refuse to exhaust it here as an exchange for everlasting life.

That brings up the supreme problem of a happy death. A happy death is a masterpiece. Our Lord labored on His masterpiece from eternity, for He is the "Lamb slain from the beginning of the world." We must labor on ours from the beginning too, for as the tree falls, there it lies.

At the moment of death, nothing will be useful to us — except God. If we have Him, then we shall recover everything in Him.

For that reason, a Christian is never in full possession of his life until the day of his death. That is why the Church calls it a *Natalitia* — birthday, the birthday into Eternal life. Eternal exile is only for those who made the earth their fatherland.

No masterpiece was ever completed in a day. It takes years for the artist to discipline his mind and hand, and then years again to chisel away the stubbornness of the marble to make the form appear. The greatest masterpiece of all — a Happy Death — must be prepared for by practice.

We learn how to die by dying, dying to our selfishness, our pride, our envy, our sloth, a thousand times a day. This is what Our Lord meant when He said: "If any man will come after me, let him . . . take up his cross daily, and follow me." We cannot die well unless we practice dying.

Then when the time comes for the last stroke, we shall be skilled in it, and we shall not be taken by surprise.

Our tower will have been completed; whether it be high or low will matter not. It only matters that we finish the plan Our Lord has given us to do. And may we all, as an old Irish saying has it: "Be in heaven half an hour before the devil knows we're dead."

ETERNAL FREEDOM

(The Seventh Word from the Cross)

"Father, into thy hands
I commend my spirit."

"FEAR YE NOT THEM that kill the body... but rather fear him that can destroy both soul and body in hell." Calvary is wrapped up in these words of Our Blessed Lord, for therein is revealed the supreme struggle of every life, — the struggle to preserve our spiritual freedom. We cannot serve both God and Mammon; we cannot save our life both for time and eternity; we cannot feast both here and hereafter; we cannot make the best of two worlds; either we will have the fast on earth and the feast in heaven, or we will have the feast here and the fast in eternity.

In order then to purchase our freedom with the glorious Christ, we may have to suffer the slavery of earth. Real freedom consists in keeping our soul our own, even though we have to lose our body to preserve it.

Sometimes it can be preserved easily, but there may arise occasions when it demands even the sacrifice of our life.

A moment may come in the life of a politician, for example, when, in order to keep his independence, he must sacrifice the ease and influence which comes with the bribe.

To every Christian in like manner, there comes the supreme moment when he must choose between temporal pleasure and eternal freedom. In order to save our souls, we must often run the risk of losing our bodies.

Our Divine Saviour had the choice put before Him on Calvary, where He kept His soul free at the cost of His life. He went down into the bodily slavery of the Cross in order to keep His soul His own.

His majesty He surrendered to the supremacy of His enemies; His hands and feet He enslaved to their nails; His body He submitted to their grave; His good name He subjugated to their scorn; His blood He poured forth captive to their lance; His comfort he subjected to their planned pain; and His life He laid down as a serf at their feet. But His spirit He kept free and for Himself.

He would not surrender it, for if He kept His freedom, He could recover everything else He had already given into their hands.

They knew that, and so they tried to enslave His Spirit by challenging His Power:

"Come down from the cross, and we will believe."

If He had Power to step down from that Cross, and yet refused, He was not a crucified prisoner, but their Judge on His Judgment Seat and their King on His Throne. If He had the Power to come down and did come down, then He would have been submitted to their will and thus become their slave.

He refused to do the human thing — to come down from the Cross. He did the divine thing, and stayed there! By so doing, He kept His soul His own.

Therefore, He could do with it whatever He pleased. All during His life, He did the things that were pleasing to His Heavenly Father; now He would do them at His death.

Laying hold of His spirit, for He was master of Himself, He sent it back again to His Father, not with a hoarse cry of rebellion, not with a weak murmur of stoical endurance, not with the quivering uncertain tones of a Hamlet debating "to be or not to be," but with the loud, strong, triumphant voice of One Who was free to go to whom He pleased, and willed to go only back home: "Father, into Thy Hands I commend My Spirit."

That was the one, inescapable, untouchable thing in His life and every life: the spirit.

We can hammer iron, because it is material; we can melt ice, because we can warm it with our fires; we can break twigs, because we can get them into our hands; but we cannot crucify Faith, we cannot melt Hope, we cannot break Charity, and we cannot murder Justice, because all these things are spiritual and therefore, beyond the power of enslavement.

In a higher sense, the soul of every man is the last and impregnable fortress of character. As long as he wills to keep his spirit his own, no one can take it away, even though they take his life.

That spirit man can freely give away or sell, for example, into the slavery of drink, but it is his own as long as he chooses to keep it.

Our Lord kept His Spirit free at the most terrible of all costs, to remind us that not even the fear of a crucifixion is a reason for stepping down from the most glorious of all liberties — the power to give our soul to God.

Unfortunately, freedom has lost its value for the modern world. It understands freedom too often as the right to do whatever you please, or the absence of constraint. This is not freedom but license, and very often anarchy.

Freedom means not the right to do what you *please*, but the right to do what we *should* in order to attain the highest and noblest ends of our nature.

An aviator is free not when he disregards the law of gravitation because it suits his fancy, but when he obeys it in order to conquer it and fly. Liberty then is a means, not an end; not a city, but a bridge.

When we say, "We want to be free," the obvious question is, "Free from what?" "Free from interruption." "Very well, but why?" "Because I want to travel to a certain place where I have business." Then freedom becomes meaningful. It implies a knowledge of a goal or a purpose.

Now human nature has a goal, namely, the using of this world as a stepping stone to the perfection of our personality, which is the enjoyment of perfect happiness.

But if we never stop to ask ourselves why we are here, or where we are going, or what is the purpose of life, then we are changing our direction, but we are not making progress; neither are we free.

If we forgot our real destiny, we cut up our lives into tiny, successive, and incomplete destinies, like a man who is lost in a forest, going first one way and then another.

If he had a single distant point, say a church steeple, beyond and outside the forest, he would be free either to go out of the forest or remain in it, and he would be making progress as he approached the church steeple.

So it is with life: if we have a fixed goal then we can make progress toward it, but it is sheer nonsense to say we are making progress if we constantly change our goal. As long as the model remains fixed, we are free to paint it, but if the model one moment is a rose and the next moment a nose, then art has lost not only its freedom but its joy.

This last and final Word on the Cross reminds us that Our Lord never lost sight of His goal and because He did not, He sacrificed everything else to keep Himself free to attain it. Surplus baggage must often be dropped in order to run freely to refuge.

That is why Our Lord told the rich man to leave his bags of gold behind, for thus he could more perfectly run the course to eternal life. Our Lord Himself dropped everything, even His life.

But He dropped it as a seed into the ground and picked it up again in the freshness of the risen life of Easter Sunday.

From this sacrifice of His life in order to keep His Spirit free from the Father, we must learn not to be overcome by the sorrows and trials and disappointments of life. The danger is that forgetting the ideal; we may concentrate more on saving our body than on saving our soul.

Too often we blame persons and things for being indifferent to our pains and aches as if they were primary. We want nature to suspend its sublime tasks, or we want persons to leave their round of duties, not just to minister to us in our necessities, but to soften us with their sympathy.

Forgetting that sometimes the work is more than the comfort, we become like those sick at sea who feel the ship should stop, hundreds should be delayed, and the port be forgotten, just to minister to their sickness.

Our Blessed Lord on the Cross might have made all nature minister to His wounds; He might have turned the Crown of thorns into a garland of roses: His nails into a sceptre, His blood into royal purple, His Cross into a golden throne, His wounds into glittering jewels. But that would have meant the ideal of sitting at the right hand of the Father in His Glory, was secondary to an immediate and temporary earthly comfort.

Then the purpose of life would have been less important than a moment in it; then the freedom of His Spirit would have been secondary to the healing of His Hands; then the higher self would have been the slave of the lower self — and that is the one thing we are bidden to avoid.

"God strengthen me to bear myself
That heaviest weight of all to bear
Inalienable weight of care.

"All others are outside myself
I lock my door and bar them out,
The turmoil, tedium, gad-about.

"I lock my door upon myself,
And bar them out; but who shall bar
Self from myself, most loathed of all?

"If I could set aside myself
And start with lightened heart upon
The road by all men overgone!

"God harden me against myself
This coward with pathetic voice
Who craves for ease, and rest, and joys.

"Myself arch-traitor to myself
My hollowest friend, my deadliest fore
My clog whatever road I go.

"Yet One there is can curb myself
Can roll the strangling load from me
Break off the yoke and set me free."

Christina Rossetti

There is no escaping the one thing necessary in the Christian life, namely saving our souls and purchasing the glorious liberty of the children of God. The crucifixion ends, but Christ endures. Sorrows pass, but we remain. Therefore we must never come down from the supreme end and purpose of life; the salvation of our souls.

Often the temptation will be strong, and the temporal advantages will seem great; but at those moments, we must recall the great difference between the solicitation of a sinful pleasure and the appeal of our heavenly destiny.

Before we have a sinful pleasure, it is attractive and appealing. After we have it, it is disgusting. It was not worth the price; we feel we were cheated and that we sold ourselves out of all proportion to our due worth, as Judas felt when he sold the Saviour for thirty pieces of silver.

But with the spiritual life, it is different. Before we have intimate union with Christ and His Cross, it seems so distasteful, so contrary to our nature, so hard and so uninviting. But after we have given ourselves over to Him, it gives a peace and a joy which surpasses all understanding. That is why so many miss Him and His joy. They stand so far away they never learn to know Him. Like the poet they ask:

"Must Thou, Designer Infinite, Char the
wood ere Thou canst limn with it?"

Francis Thompson
"The Hound of Heaven"

Must the wood be subject to fire before we can paint with it as charcoal? Is death the condition of life? Is the discipline of study the path to knowledge? Are long hours of tedious practice, the road to the thrill of music? Must we lose our lives in time in order to save them for eternity? Yes. That is the answer.

But it is not so hard as it seems, for, as St. Paul tells us: "The sorrows of this life are not worthy to be compared to the joys that are to come." How often as little children, when our little toys were broken, we thought life was no longer worth living, for the universe, was in ruins; and then, surveying the wreck which seemed so hopeless, we cried ourselves to sleep.

May not those once great sorrows which faded into insignificance with maturity be but the symbol of the trivialities of our present burdens, compared to the joys which await us in the mansions of the Father's House?

Only let us not be fooled by those who say human life has no purpose, and who, in the language of a scientist, say that life is like a lit candle and that when the candle is done the flame goes out, and that is the end of us all.

But what this scientist forgot to tell us is that light is not something in the candle, but something which emanates from it; something associated with matter but separable and distinct from it. For even when the candle has burned out, the light continues to emit itself at the rate of 186,000 miles a second, beyond the moon and stars, beyond the Pleiades, the nebulas of Andromeda and continues to do so as long as the universe endures.

And so when the candle of our life burns low, may we have kept our soul so free, that like a flame it will leap upwards to the Great Fire at which it was enkindled, and never stop until its light meets that Heavenly Light which ages ago came to this world as its Light, to teach us all to say at the end of our earthly pilgrimage here, as He said at the close of His: "Father, into Thy Hands I commend My Spirit."

ACKNOWLEDGMENTS

To the members of the Archbishop Fulton John Sheen Foundation in Peoria, Illinois. In particular, to the Most Rev. Daniel R. Jenky, C.S.C., Bishop of Peoria, for your leadership and fidelity to the cause of Sheen's canonization and the creation of this book.

www.archbishopsheencause.org

To the staff at Sophia Institute Press for their invaluable assistance in sharing the writings of Archbishop Fulton J. Sheen to a new generation of readers.

www.sophiainstitute.com

To the volunteers at the Archbishop Fulton J. Sheen Mission Society of Canada: your motto "Unless Souls are Saved, Nothing is Saved", speaks to the reality that Jesus Christ came into the world to make salvation available to all souls.

www.archbishopfultonjsheenmissionsocietyofcanada.org

To the good folks at 'Bishop Sheen Today'. We value your guidance, support, and prayers in helping us to share the wisdom of Archbishop Fulton J. Sheen. Your apostolic work of sharing his audio and video presentations along with his many writings to a worldwide audience is very much appreciated.

www.bishopsheentoday.com

And lastly, to Archbishop Fulton J. Sheen, whose teachings on Our Lord's Passion and His Seven Last Words continue to inspire me to love God more and to appreciate the gift of the Church. May we be so blessed as to imitate Archbishop Sheen's love for the saints, the sacraments, the Eucharist, and the Blessed Virgin Mary. May the Good Lord grant him a very high place in heaven!

ABOUT THE AUTHOR
Fulton J. Sheen
(1895–1979)

ARCHBISHOP SHEEN, best known for his popularly televised and syndicated television program, Life is Worth Living, is held today as one of Catholicism's most widely recognized figures of the twentieth century.

Fulton John Sheen, born May 8, 1895, in El Paso, Illinois was raised and educated in the Roman Catholic faith. Originally named Peter John Sheen, he came to be known as a young boy by his mother's maiden name, Fulton. He was ordained a priest of the Diocese of Peoria at St. Mary's Cathedral in Peoria, IL on September 20, 1919.

Following his ordination, Sheen studied at the Catholic University of Louvain, where he earned a doctorate in philosophy in 1923. That same year, he received the Cardinal Mercier Prize for International Philosophy, becoming the first-ever American to earn this distinction.

Upon returning to America, after varied and extensive work throughout Europe, Sheen continued to preach and teach theology and philosophy from 1927 to 1950, at the Catholic University of America in Washington DC.

Beginning in 1930, Sheen hosted a weekly Sunday night radio broadcast called 'The Catholic Hour'. This broadcast captured many devoted listeners, reportedly drawing an audience of four million people every week for over twenty years.

In 1950, he became the National Director of the Society for the Propagation of the Faith, raising funds to support missionaries. During the sixteen years that he held this position, millions of dollars were raised to support the missionary activity of the Church. These efforts influenced tens of millions of people all over the world, bringing them to know Christ and his Church. In addition, his preaching and personal example brought about many converts to Catholicism.

In 1951, Sheen was appointed Auxiliary Bishop of the Archdiocese of New York. That same year, he began hosting his television program 'Life is Worth Living', which lasted for six years.

In the course of its run, that program competed for airtime with popular television programs hosted by the likes of Frank Sinatra and Milton Berle. Sheen's program held its own, and in 1953, just two years after its debut, he won an Emmy Award for "Most Outstanding Television Personality." Fulton Sheen credited the Gospel writers - Matthew, Mark, Luke, and John - for their valuable contribution to his success. Sheen's television show ran until 1957, boasting as many as thirty million weekly viewers.

In the Fall of 1966, Sheen was appointed Bishop of Rochester, New York. During that time, Bishop Sheen hosted another television series, 'The Fulton Sheen Program' which ran from 1961 to 1968, closely modeling the format of his 'Life is Worth Living' series.

After nearly three years as Bishop of Rochester, Fulton Sheen resigned and was soon appointed by Pope Paul VI as Titular Archbishop of the See of Newport, Wales. This new appointment allowed Sheen the flexibility to continue preaching.

Another claim to fame was Bishop Sheen's annual Good Friday homilies, which he preached for fifty-eight consecutive years at St. Patrick's Cathedral in New York City, and elsewhere. Sheen also led numerous retreats for priests and religious, preaching at conferences all over the world.

When asked by Pope St. Pius XII how many converts he had made, Sheen responded, "Your Holiness, I have never counted them. I am always afraid that if I did count them, I might think I made them, instead of the Lord."

Sheen was known for being approachable and down to earth. He used to say, "If you want people to stay as they are, tell them what they want to hear. If you want to improve them, tell them what they should know." This he did, not only in his preaching but also through his numerous books and articles. His book titled 'Peace of Soul' was sixth on the New York Times best-seller list.

Three of Sheen's great loves were: the missions and the propagation of the faith; the Holy Mother of God and the Eucharist.

He made a daily holy hour of prayer before the Blessed Sacrament. It was from Jesus Himself that he drew strength and inspiration to preach the gospel, and in the Presence of Whom that he prepared his homilies. "I beg [Christ] every day to keep me strong physically and alert mentally, in order to preach His gospel and proclaim His Cross and Resurrection," he said. "I am so happy doing this that I sometimes feel that when I come to the good Lord in Heaven, I will take a few days' rest and then ask Him to allow me to come back again to this earth to do some more work."

His contributions to the Catholic Church are numerous and varied, ranging from educating in classrooms, churches, and homes, to preaching over a nationally-publicized radio show, and two television programs, as well as penning over sixty written works. Archbishop Fulton J. Sheen had a gift for communicating the Word of God in the most pure, simple way. His strong background in philosophy helped him to relate to everyone in a highly personalized manner. His timeless messages continue to have great relevance today. His goal was to inspire everyone to live a God-centered life with the joy and love that God intended.

On October 2, 1979, Archbishop Sheen received his greatest accolade, when Pope St. John Paul II embraced him at St. Patrick's Cathedral in New York City. The Holy Father said to him, "You have written and spoken well of the Lord Jesus. You are a loyal son of the Church."

The good Lord called Fulton Sheen home on December 9, 1979. His television broadcasts now available through various media, and his books, extend his earthly work of winning souls for Christ. Sheen's cause for canonization was opened in 2002. In 2012, Pope Benedict XVI declared him 'Venerable', and in July of 2019, Pope Francis formally approved the miracle necessary for Sheen's beatification and canonization process to move forward. The time and date for the church to declare Archbishop Fulton J. Sheen a saint is in God's hands.

J.M.J

Books Available Through Bishop Sheen Today Publishing

The Seven Last Words

Calvary and the Mass

The Holy Hour Prayer Book

The Cross and the Beatitudes

The Cross and the Crisis

Missions and the World Crisis

The Seven Last Words of Christ Explained

Father, Forgive Them for They Know Not What They Do.

This Day Thou Shall Be with Me in Paradise

Woman Behold Your Son; Behold Your Mother

My God! My God! Why Hast Thou Forsaken Me?

I Thirst

It is Finished

The Rainbow of Sorrow

Love One Another

The Divine Verdict

God Love You

The Seven Last Words Explained

The Priest Is Not His Own

The Cross and the Crib

Philosophies at War

Seven Words to the Cross

Seven Pillars of Peace

Love One Another

Seven Words of Jesus & Mary

Victory Over Vice

The Seven Virtues

For God and Country

God and War

Father Into Your Hands I Commend My Spirit

Liberty, Equality and Fraternity

www.bishopsheentoday.com

www.ingramcontent.com/pod-product-compliance
Lightning Source LLC
Chambersburg PA
CBHW031218120626
46545CB00003B/894